The Oxford Piano Method

T0088437

PIANO TIME JAZZ

Book 2

Pauline Hall

MUSIC DEPARTMENT

OXFORD
UNIVERSITY PRESS

OXFORD
UNIVERSITY PRESS

Great Clarendon Street, Oxford OX2 6DP, England
198 Madison Avenue, New York, NY10016, USA

Oxford University Press is a department of the University of Oxford.
It furthers the University's aim of excellence in research, scholarship,
and education by publishing worldwide

Oxford is a registered trade mark of Oxford University Press
in the UK and in certain other countries

© Oxford University Press 1999

Database right Oxford University Press (maker)

First published 1999

All rights reserved. No part of this publication may be reproduced,
stored in a retrieval system, or transmitted, in any form or by any means,
without the prior permission in writing of Oxford University Press,
or as expressly permitted by law. Enquiries concerning reproduction
outside the scope of the above should be sent to the Music Copyright
Department, Oxford University Press, at the address above

Permission to perform the works in this anthology in public
(except in the course of divine worship) should normally be obtained
from the Performing Right Society Ltd. (PRS), 29/33 Berners Street,
London W1T 3AB, or its affiliated Societies in each country throughout
the world, unless the owner or the occupier of the premises
being used holds a licence from the Society

Permission to make a recording must be obtained in advance
from the Mechanical Copyright Protection Society Ltd. (MCPS),
Elgar House, 41 Streatham High Road, London SW16 1ER,
or its affiliated Societies in each country throughout the world

24

ISBN 0-19-372734-X 978-0-19-372734-2

Illustrations by Andy Hammond

Music and text origination by
Barnes Music Engraving Ltd., East Sussex
Printed in Great Britain on acid-free paper by
Halstan & Co. Ltd., Amersham, Bucks.

Contents

Reggae stamp	4
Warm starry nights	5
Clear water	6
Late at night	7
High Street blues	8
Waltz for Alice	10
Snowball rag	11
Star gazing	12
Chase in the dark	13
Three-quarter time	14
Funfair	16
Ol' man boogie blues	17
Head in the clouds	18
Moody Max	19
Go with the flow	20
Tango Argentina	22
Railroad blues	23
Whistle stop	24
Cat's eyes	25
Polka dots	26
Round the bend	28
Promise!	29
Warm up	30
Lively lion	32

Reggae stamp

FIONA MACARDLE

Warm starry nights

STEPHEN DURO

Slow beguine

mf

f

ten.

mf

p

Clear water

DAVID BLACKWELL

Late at night

FIONA MACARDLE

High Street blues

ALAN BULLARD

sfz
sfz
HIGH STREET

Waltz for Alice

ROY STRATFORD

Snowball rag

FIONA MACARDLE

Star gazing

ALAN BULLARD

Chase in the dark

DAVID BLACKWELL

Three-quarter time

ALAN BULLARD

mf
2
mp
5
5
1
f

Funfair

PAULINE HALL

Ol' man boogie blues

PETER GRITTON

Ponderous, but rhythmic

mp

mf

mp

mf

p

poco rit.

Head in the clouds

ALAN BULLARD

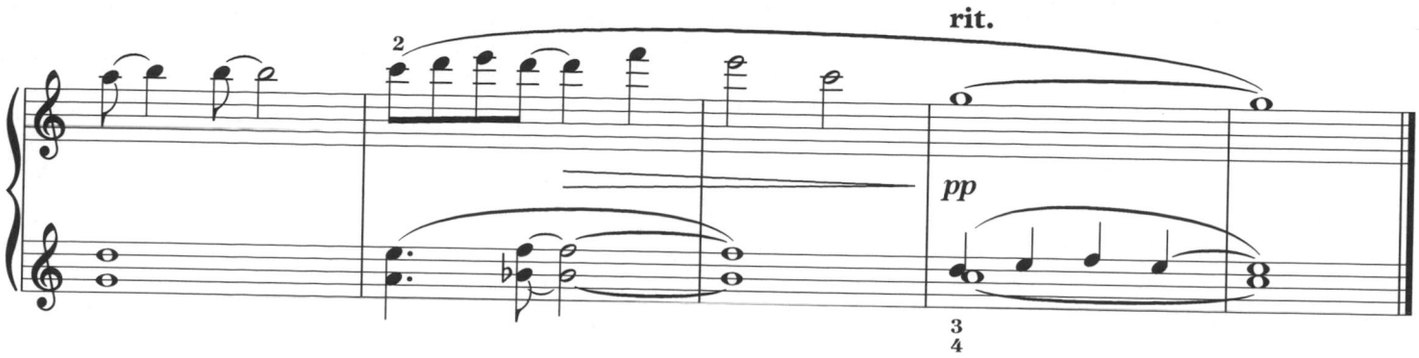

Moody Max

DAVID BLACKWELL

Go with the flow

ALAN BULLARD

p espress.
1
1
mp
1
mf
p

Tango Argentina

PAULINE HALL

Railroad blues

DAVID BLACKWELL

Whistle stop

PAUL DRAYTON

Cat's eyes

DAVID BLACKWELL

Polka dots

DAVID BLACKWELL

mf
f
2

JAZZ BAND TONIGHT

Round the bend

ALAN BULLARD

Promise!

RODERICK SKEAPING

This isn't as hard as it looks! Use the words to help you with the rhythm and say them in time before you start to play.

Warm up

ROY STRATFORD

f
mp
f

Lively lion